MW01248265

Words I Never Said

Jenna Thompson

BookLeaf
Publishing
India | USA | UK

Presentation by *BookLeaf Publishing*

Web: www.bookleafpub.com

E-mail: info@bookleafpub.com

ISBN: 9789357448192

First edition 2022

DEDICATION

To every person who has shown me love, but
especially: Ma, Mimi, Karen, Mrs. Becky, and
Denise. And to my Mom, who tried her best.

Found Freedom

I knew liberation
when the claws
you had extended
into me, let go.
I found independence
In the lines
of my face
when I stared
in the mirror.
My buried autonomy
rose from it's grave
rearing it's head
shedding the guilt
and fear of living
that lives inside me.
The emancipation
of my sorrowful soul
is learning to survive
under the influence
of pure happiness.
Tell me, do you know
what it means to find
comfort in captivity
rather than freedom?

Talk About Loss

Some people talk about loss
By vowing silence as their companion.
Letting it habituate in their chest
Until there is no beginning or end.

Some people talk about loss
With halting sentences of grief
Trying to hold back a tsunami
Of pain and bitterness in their souls.

Some people talk about loss
With pride seeping through the pores
Of the words they let fall
Fron the poison of their lips.

Some people talk about loss
With intermittent laughs
And halting stanzas of beauty
Teeming with love between the spaces.

Some people talk about loss
Letting the rising anger
Swell to its ultimate crescendo
And crash into a cliff of despair.

Some people talk about loss
As if the person stood in the room
Whispering in the ear of the speaker
The secrets they kept to the grave.

Some people talk about loss
And their sincerity falls flat
The wrong tune on a brass instrument
Meant to be played on a string.

Some people talk about loss
Displaying proudly the feathers
Of spun gold, sifting between the
Cracks and crevices of the deceased.

Some people talk about loss,
And some never talk at all.

Pieces

I have torn myself to pieces
Trying to understand the ways
In which you've destroyed me.
How do I heal from a complete tear?
I am no longer attached to who
I was in the long, forgotten past.
Yet, I find myself wanting to
Love her from closer than the mirror.
I am bound behind, a simple reflection
Of that person people are used to
seeing.

Whole

The mirror is good at reflections,
And hatred is all I see.
I'm asking for your embrace;
I'm asking you to love me.

That person in my image
Is broken beyond repair;
But, take my broken pieces;
Make it beauty beyond compare.

I never ask for much, you see
A simple task to be tended to,
And I promise to be quiet,
To never take up too much room.

So, if you can, take this puzzle
These pieces of me so sharp
Put them together in some semblance
So I am whole and of good heart.

Your Soul

Why do I hold so tightly to your soul?
You're so deep inside of me
I don't know how to let you go.

Sad Soul

I have always had this broken
Sort of sadness inside of me.
Some days, its silence rings
In the thoughts of my mind.
Other days, the words it speaks
Play like a mantra I never forget.
I have asked it to leave me
Time after time, but it stays.
And now, it's become a friend.
Reliable and loyal, when I am alone.
I wish I had the heart to let it go.
Maybe then I wouldn't feel
So vulnerable every time someone
Decides to criticize who I am.
It is a part of me I cannot deny.
And to my dying day, I will
Forever be some sort of sad soul.

Entities

Sadness visits me by the midnight moon.
Pain nests itself between my ribs.
Anger prefers the roost of my shoulder.
Disappointment lies between my eyes.
Sorrow is an old friend I wish would leave.
Anxiety tries to put all blame on me.
Fear settles in the cracks of my skin.
I have known these entities for so long,
That they laugh when I try to discard them.

Ocean of Anger

There are moments in which
The anger of my soul is a vast
Unexplored ocean of emotion.
Most days I feign ignorance
To the existence of it in my chest.
And other days I am submerged;
The salt making the pressure
On my diaphragm too much.
And just like the deep waters
I go on for thousands of feet
Down into the vestiges of parts
of me I'd rather forget about.
Some dwell on the depths of
Themselves and never leave.
Some walk away till they burn
From the exposure to light.
I am neither. Some say I am
The light of my soul, and others
I am desperate to be calm
In the waters of my broken being.
And some days, I am cursed to be
One foot in, and one foot out.

Faces within Me

I searched for familiarity in the faces
Of silence, loneliness, and pain.
And they looked back with an intensity
That stole the ambition out of me.
How do you explain to people
That these things are more of a home
Then the place in which you rest your feet?

They have stayed with me for a lifetime
Giving me painful comfort in times
When I was broken beyond repair.
And yet you asked me, why keep them?
Do you get rid of a favorite teddy bear
Because you're too old to sleep with it?
No, you take comfort in its softness.
And so these three that have been with me, were
handed down by generation?
How could I refuse them a place within me?

Mama?

Where did you go, Mama?
I cannot find you here.
The whisper of my words
Lost between my tears.

Can you hear me, Mama?
Sometimes I need you here
Your voice I miss so often
I know I feel you near.

Can you hug me, Mama?
So often I am alone
I bare it well, they tell me
Assurance in their tones.

Are you proud of me, Mama?
I whisper to your grave
And in that moment of sorrow
I lose courage that makes me brave

Are you up there, Mama?
I say underneath my breath
I yearn for her smile and warmth
With all the love in my chest

Wait for me Mama?
I request in a small voice
Crowding my heart with silence
I give her no other choice

A daughter's love is vast and deep
Because it holds secrets we don't speak

Loss and Grief

Loss is subjective by nature,
And I am the person that hefts it
To my back with each passing day.

As people walk so easily away from me
I great loss as an ally instead of enemy
Because I am too tired to argue with it.

Do not be fooled by Grief's intentions
Because it will strip you of feeling
And leave horrifying numbness in place.

Just You

I searched the crowd of faces
For some indirect association
Of the image I had of you.
In the man tapping his foot
I found your impatience.
In the baby wailing its cry
I found your abused ambition.
In the woman with dark circled eyes
I found the reason you chose death.
In the sister watching her brother
I found your hidden resentment.
In the pair of laughing lovers
I found your misshapen desire.
In the arguing of the older couple
I found your willingness to survive.
And in the picture in my pocket
So carefully creased and forgotten
I found a picture of you. Just you.

Memory Never Forgets

The problem is the memory never forgets.
Like the old black and white films
I am cursed to watch but never speak.
They move with exaggerated expression
Beating against veins in my brain
Trying to take me away, its suppression.
But I digress. These melodies that play in the
Scenes from not so long ago remind me
Of a carousel of horses, forever going in
A direction that never quite stops the pain.
They are meant to be a map to escape,
But instead they are a pin point straight
To the strings of my heart, thrumming
In beat to the drums that bang in the
background. I beg for the screeching in
My head to stop, to find another body
To antagonize into a sea of hopelessness.
I get lost in the current as it waves over me
Stealing the oxygen from my lungs so easily
That I begin to believe that my fate has always
Been this very moment in which I give up.
Thrashing and treading I make it back for

A single intake of air, and back under
To begin the process over and over until
This life finally takes all of it from my chest.

Your Performance

I fell between the pieces of the
Cracked reflection you buried
To hide the truth in your soul;
And there, I discovered webs
Of tangled truths and lies
Ones you cannot see or believe;
And those that you use to veil
The facade of who you are.
The coldness of the image you
Projected to the outside world
Proved to be overwhelmed by
The heated anger that left
Third-degree burns on my skin;
And like many, I bore scars
From the days I spent trying
To comprehend the utter hatred
You felt for others around you.
Where many people only saw
The outside in to what you showed,
I held a front row seat, bound
To the masks you put forth, and
You deserved a Grammy for
The show-stopping performance
You've been giving for years.
The ligature marks on my wrists

Were the only evidence of it.
I wanted to despise you with all
Of the emotions bursting beneath
The layers of my skin, and yet
I found myself clapping, awed
By your ability to portray such
Perfection in the face of everything.
I wanted to throw you off the stage
And yet I threw flowers for you instead.

I found myself

I found my anger in the broken pieces of my soul, begging me to put the puzzle back together in some semblance of being whole.

I found bitterness nested in the attic of my mind, taking to the rafters in an attempt to escape the chaos of my memories.

I found disappointment lining the edges of my heart, sewn into the fabric so deeply that pulling it apart would cause irreparable damage.

I found sorrow bleeding inside the middle of my body, and like poison it colored every hope I had come to own in my life.

I found frustration nailed to the foundation of my beginning, as if each situation had somehow taken the patience I had so diligently gathered.

I found desperation between the lines of my palms, as if for every moment I worked to be better, those around me only saw a burden meant to be left behind.

I found myself in the tattered trenches of memories, lost in a war zone of relationships that have destroyed my confidence.

I found myself, and I struggled to my feet, and I began the long trek towards home.

I found myself, and though quiet, I rejoiced.

Obstacle

You are the last obstacle.
The wall between me and
A door that I never left open.
And I'm not sure how to traverse
The terrain of anger and spite,
Of the disappointment that lingers
So heavily upon my bruised heart.
You stand like a sentinel
Protecting the vestiges of me
That I'm not sure how to overcome
While guarding the remnants
Of the sorrow that sits in my chest.
I feel cracked open, staring at you.
It could lead to my healing
Or it could shatter the last
Of the control I desperately hold
Onto for the sake of those around me.
The strength I find in myself
Is simply what's been left behind
By others who drop it so easily.
I see their bravery, and I hold
Tight to the insanity inside my chest.
I take what they give in that I
Might find the same courage

To face the demons hiding
Inside the portions of me
I block from the rest of the world.
You stand between me and the door,
And I won't fight you for that,
Because I only have room for one brawl,
And it will take everything from within
This tattered being to keep myself whole.
One day, when you're gone,
I'll be able to wrestle myself
Into some semblance of a cracked puzzle,
Until then, just keep me safe,
Even if I break in the process.

I am not You

I am not broken
Simply bent in a shape
That takes all of my energy
To keep it from snapping.

I am not burned
Simply a survivor
Of smoking inhaled
Insults mean to crush me.

I am not bruised
Simply discolored skin
Draped over bones
Without an ounce of softness.

I am not cracked
Simply in pieces
From where they
Sliced me too deep.

I am not torn
Simply sewn together
With veiled words of webbed
Lies that torment me

I am not weak
Simply zapped of energy
Too exhausted to hold up
This body of white ash.

I am not sorry
Simply too tired
To refute the implications
Of your veiled threats.

I am not real
Simply living amongst
The living dead that
Choose materials over people.

I am not you
Simply a person of
Profound sadness
And happiness in one.

Burning

I was raised to believe in you.
To lift you up beyond the clouds,
To observe your place on high
Inside the boxes of our minds.
But you cursed me, when I was young.
And I watched you burn in
The shallows of your own chaos;
Forced to see you drown in the
Scant inches of bitterness left behind
By those that took your lifeblood.
My faith in you withered like
The trees falling victim to flame;
Building ash into the atmosphere
Until it drags the breath from my lungs.
And it means you get to keep
Taking each inch of me to keep
For yourself, and I am nothing.
I hold back, layering my own embrace
In defense of the army you have
Coming for me; and I have to surrender
Watching your rage of terror journey
To the depths of my identity
And force from my lips the praise
You so desperately need to feel satisfaction.
This life holds for me no beginning

Only an end to which I fall prey.
To your wasted efforts of "giving"
So deep breaths, in and out.
Remember to leave her behind,
Or else you will begin another lie.

Silence

She rolled hope around her mouth
Like syllables aching on her tongue
To burst forth and scream her vengeance

And still she was Silent.

She felt the rhythm in her steps
Falter in the light of noon day
Dragging her from the destination

And still she was Silent.

The vibrations in her larynx
Caught the edges of her throat
Begging for mercy, to rectify her ache.

And still she was Silent.

She mimicked her hands in display
Of what she hope would make language
And no one could comprehend her motions

And still she was Silent.

She watched those she loved walk away

Twin peaks of moisture washing her face
Shrieking violence into her lungs

And still she was Silent.

You see, no one listened like Silence
No one cared for her like Silence
No one gave a damm, except Silence.

And so she gave herself to it, without a word.

I begged you not to go

I remember moments of joy
When you twined your fingers in mine
And laughed without abandon
And I begged you not to go.

I remember minutes spent next to you
While your breath slowly ceased
And you slept with all the tension
And I begged you not to go.

I remember days of peaceful contentment
When you and I would never stop
Talking about my potential future
And I begged you not to go.

I remember the frustrating night
When you stalked me out in the dark
Screaming that I needed to understand
And I begged you not to go.

I remember gentle hugs and kisses
When I was young and the world

Was a place full of endless possibility
And I begged you not to go.

I remember the moment it was stolen
When you laid your head on me
And cried for a loss I didnt understand
And I begged you not to go.

I remember being so filled with joy
When I would run home to be with you
To imitate the very image of you
And I begged you not to go.

I remember the silence of that room
When I watched you slip away
Endless moments of pure agony
And I begged you not to go.

You see, I remember everything
All the memories of us combined
With bitterness and joy in one
And now I have to let you go.

Set Free

Remembering the good times,
Rejoicing in beloved memories,
She waits for us in Heaven,
Singing joyous melodies.
No longer suffering on Earth,
Or bearing strenuous health,
Her mind has been set free,
In heaven she's attained her wealth.
She laughs with whole abandon,
Her suffering away with the wind,
Her heart lives on in everyone,
Even if this is where She ends.
In moments of sadness,
And moments of grief,
Even in a Journey so long,
She has found her peace.

Printed in the USA
CPSIA information can be obtained
at www.ICGtesting.com
LVHW050306091224
798643LV00006B/1466